Norsk Høstfest
Heritage Comes Alive

by Lori & Jim Olson
Photography by Clayton Wolt

American & World Geographic Publishing

Above: Chet Atkins and Crystal Gayle enjoy the Scandinavian-American Hall of Fame Banquet.

Right: Music spills over into all areas of the festival.

Title page: Opening a door to the past.

Front cover: Hannah Beth Bulla of the Bulla Family.

ISBN 1-56037-078-5

Text © 1995 Lori & Jim Olson
Photography © 1995 Clayton Wolt
© 1995 Norsk Høstfest Association and
American & World Geographic Publishing

Write for our catalog:

American & World Geographic Publishing
P.O. Box 5630, Helena, MT 59604

Printed in U.S.A.

An artisan plies his trade at Høstfest.

Above: Vikings in search of loot.

Facing page: Strolling musicians liven up every corner of the festival.

Contents

Above: Lefse! Hot off the griddle.

Right: Everyone is Scandinavian at Høstfest time.

Facing page: Chet Reiten, President of the Norsk Høstfest Association, welcoming attendees.

Foreword

by Chester M. Reiten, President, Norsk Høstfest

The Høstfest is a folk festival designed to be a time for fun, fellowship, and inspiration—a time to meet old friends of yesteryear and to make new ones.

The theme of Høstfest is modeled after the great pleasures and memories of a small rural town on a Saturday night, a time when family values were strong and friendly camaraderie flowed between friends and neighbors.

The best antidote available to restore the United States to its role as an unparalleled inspiration to the world is to return to the principles that guided our early settlers. America has been the most copied and admired nation in the world because it was built on the sound and sober values of our forefathers.

These values of heritage also are the foundation on which this Høstfest is built.

Hopefully, through the influence of the Høstfest and similar groups, the philosophies and ethics of our great past, such as faith in God, the work ethic, honesty, responsibility, and respect for the rights of others, will again be the dominant force in our nation.

The *fun* of this festival has never faced a more important job than to display and honor the noble values which our country holds dear.

Those precious values, bought with the very lives of our ancestors, have prevailed up to now. It is our responsibility and our privilege to honor the past, to prevail in an uncertain present, and to break new ground in the exciting future.

One of the favorites among Høstfest-goers—Swedish meatballs.

*Left: Chet and Joy Reiten
and Norwegian tour
operator Erling Skogvold.*

*Below: The good taste of
Høstfest.*

Right: Parade of Flags onstage at the Great Hall of the Vikings.

Below: Fjord horses from Canada. Larry Boe is the owner.

Facing page: A kota, *used by the Sami people living in northern Scandinavia.*

Norsk Høstfest
Heritage Comes Alive

What do you call an event that brings together thousands of people from around the continent and across the ocean, each seeking his or her own style of fun? What do you call a place that magically transports people from the wide open prairies of North Dakota to the fjords, mountains, and villages of Norway, Sweden, Denmark, Finland, and Iceland? What do you call a festival that's built on the values and traditions of generations past, that inspires people to search for their families' roots?

The answer? The Norsk Høstfest.

Norsk Høstfest is a festival that offers people from all walks of life a unique, memorable experience. Høstfest makes patrons swear they've stepped not into a huge expanse of cement and girders known as All Seasons Arena in Minot, North Dakota, but into their past—into a world where everyone is a friend, whether from days gone by or future, and where the good in life is celebrated. Høstfest allows visitors a chance to pause and taste the food they remember from childhood, or dance to music once played Saturday nights in town squares in America or Norway or Sweden, or see a crafter creating a design that grand-mothers and great-grandmothers once lovingly produced, or just sit and soak in the sight of others enjoying themselves.

It's all here—all waiting to be discovered—the Norsk Høstfest.

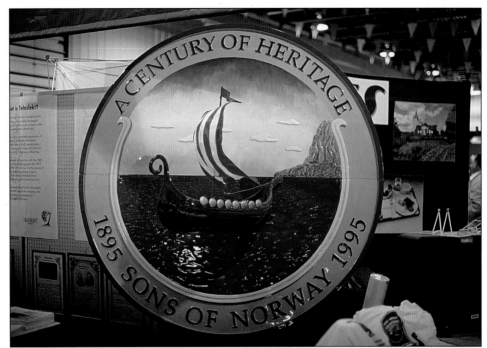

Right: A proud celebration.

Below: Yet another don't-miss for the power shopper.

Left: Just one of the many opportunities to twinkle your toes at Høstfest.

Below: And did we say there are lots of happy people and plenty of food?

Above: The Norway Lutheran Church near Denbigh, North Dakota.

Facing page: Tore Grindem, a mounted policeman from Oslo, Norway.

Humble Beginnings

How did it all begin, this small ethnic celebration turned internationally-known event—this "happening" that inspires thousands to travel to Minot, North Dakota, for five nights and four days every October?

While it's tempting to claim that Høstfest, as the huge festival it is today, is the result of a grand design laid down at the beginning—that's not the case. In reality, North America's largest Scandinavian festival began as a modest attempt to expand upon existing gatherings in and around the northwestern North Dakota city of Minot—and as a small seed of an idea in the minds of Chester (Chet) Reiten and a few of his friends.

During the mid-1970s (and still today) food and crafts bazaars were popular events at many of the Lutheran churches so prevalent on the prairies of the region. And because being both Lutheran and North Dakotan often meant also being of Scandinavian descent, signs of that ethnic heritage often flavored the events. One particularly popular bazaar, a sesquicentennial celebration organized by the Bethany, Zion, Christ, and First Lutheran churches of Minot featured festive *bunads* (Norway's traditional costume—pronounced BOO-nads), displays and demonstrations of Norwegian arts and crafts, and, of course, plenty of food. That bazaar was well attended, and a report on the event ended with the rhetorical question, "Why can't this type of celebration be continued?" Reiten and his friends took the question seriously—why couldn't this type of celebration be continued?—and the seed of an idea began to take root.

Around the same time, members of the local Sons of Norway chapter were also

discussing the possibility of an event that would put all the features of the popular church bazaars under one roof. The members' ideas and the developing plans of Reiten and his friends were merged and, in 1977, the foundation was laid for the first Høstfest, ultimately held in October of 1978.

And so it began. "First Annual Norsk Høstfest," proclaimed the modest red and white poster, "October 27 & 28 • All Seasons Arena • Everyone Welcome." The advertisement promised special prizes from Norway, a *rømmegrøt* eating contest, and, "Lutefisk, meatball, and lefse suppers"—all for an admission price of one dollar.

While not many people by today's Høstfest standards came to that first festival (estimates cover a wide range, from 1,000 to 6,000), at the time it seemed like a deluge. Pamela Alme Davy, current executive director of Høstfest, remembers how popular the event was. In those days Davy had no official connection to the Høstfest—just strong Scandinavian genes. She and her husband, mother and father set out for All Seasons Arena that Friday night, hungry for the lye-soaked (honest!) codfish known as lutefisk, but upon arrival were turned away at the door of a room filled to capacity. "I'd been to many lutefisk dinners and not once had I been shooed away because it was too full! I knew then that there was something special going on."

That first year's entire Høstfest was held in what is now the Great Hall of the Vikings (see map, page 22). It included some craft displays, music, and—the

pièce de résistance—food, which was provided then, as it is to a substantial degree today, by local churches. Reiten admits that the first year the big draw was the lutefisk supper, but he knew that that first festival was offering so much more. The idea, says Reiten, was (and still is) to "take people back to the time when everyone went into town on Saturday night. They'd eat, shop, dance, and just chat with their friends and neighbors."

That "small town Saturday night" atmosphere may be what first-year Høstfest-goers experienced when the festival filled only one hall, but even today, with more than 200,000 square feet of wall-to-wall excitement, people at Høstfest still think they're back in the town square—it's just that the town has grown a bit!

Among those attending the first Høstfest in 1978 was Ellen Lovdahl of McGregor, North Dakota. She had made North Dakota her home only four years before that first festival, moving from Norway where she was born and raised. Lovdahl had noticed a small advertisement in the Minot newspaper for Høstfest and she, her husband, and infant son headed for the All Seasons Arena to see what this ethnic festival was all about. The *bunads*, the authentic Norwegian food, and

Above: The voices of the Nittedal Choir from Norway fill the Great Hall.

Top: Looking for treasures in the Viking market.

Facing page: Everyone helps celebrate the coming alive of heritage.

the general atmosphere of the Høstfest stirred memories of home for Lovdahl and, she said, "I've been hooked ever since." (So hooked, in fact, that she has attended every Høstfest except one—and then she was visiting Norway!) The Norwegian immigrant said she realized immediately that heritage was an important part of life for the people in this area, so many of whom have family trees with roots burrowing deep into the heart of Norway.

National Danish Gymnastics Team performs at Scandinavian-American Hall of Fame Banquet.

Another thing Lovdahl noticed during Høstfest was the role volunteerism plays in the event—she talked to many people who were performing various tasks without pay. That "willing-and-able" spirit Lovdahl observed is something festival president Chet Reiten credits with helping to make the event grow year after year. "I'm always surprised at people's willingness to volunteer to help make Høstfest work," said Reiten. "Businesses donate workers, paying their salaries while they help at the festival. People even take vacation time to volunteer—they can honestly say, 'I helped make it happen!'" (An interesting statistic: The number of volunteers needed to stage a '90s Høstfest exceeds the total number of people who attended the first festival—about 8,000 volunteer passes are issued each year.)

Aside from the masses of volunteers, there is an *individual* Reiten credits with fueling the big jump in the festival's popularity beginning in its second year: entertainer Myron Floren. Floren, a native South Dakotan, gained fame as an accordionist on TV's "The Lawrence Welk Show" and is, by the way, of Scandinavian descent. His music captures the spirit of the Midwest, the goodness of its people, and the rhythm of its prairies. "When I got Myron Floren to come, and I saw the response of the crowds, I knew this thing would work," said Reiten. The enthusiastic crowds would convince Høstfest organizers to add more big-name entertainers to subsequent festivals, but those in charge would never forget the man who sparked the early success—Floren has been back for every Høstfest except one since his first appearance in 1979.

By the time the second Høstfest was history, it became evident that "this thing" *would* work. Høstfest No. 2, October 26 and 27, 1979, was attended by an estimated 12,000 people—at least double, and perhaps *ten times* the attendance of the inaugural event (remember, there was a wide-ranging attendance estimate for the first year). It was obvious the word was out: Norsk Høstfest was worth marking on the calendar.

Something else was obvious to Reiten: big talent will draw big crowds—it

Above: Can you pick out the living doll?

Top: Mayor of Minot, Orlin Backes, presents world-renowned musician and comic Victor Borge the key to the city. Danish Chocolate Kitchen chef Erik Ejsenhardt looks on in approval.

Left: Dancing breaks out all over Høstfest.

was a message that got through to Pam Davy as well. In that second year, Davy had volunteered to help with the festival and was assigned to escort Myron Floren around town during his stay. Their day started at 10:00 A.M. when she and fellow volunteer Jim Johnson picked up Floren at the airport. It continued with autograph signings, performances, and interviews until, at nearly 11:00 P.M., Davy realized that they had not taken time all day to eat. "We went to North Hill Bowl restaurant and when we walked in, people practically stood on tables for a chance to get Myron's autograph—it was at least another hour before we could eat. A couple of ladies called me to their table, and when I told them I had been with Myron all day, they asked for *my* autograph too!"

For the next few years, Høstfest grew steadily, attracting 16,000 people in 1980, 18,000 the following year, and an estimated 20,000 in 1982. And while turnstiles were revolving more frequently, the sphere of influence of this ethnic festival was also expanding. People were coming not just from Minot or North Dakota, but also from several other states and Canadian provinces as well—and even from the Nordic nations. Indeed, in 1983, Høstfest scored a dazzling coup when Princess Astrid of Norway paid a royal visit. The princess was then the most important Scandinavian dignitary to grace Høstfest with a personal visit—it was a big happening in the Minot area and helped put Høstfest on the map back in Norway as well. Such a VIP was Her Highness, that the Norwegian Consul General from Minneapolis spent a few days in Minot prior to the festival to make sure Høstfest staff members who were to have contact with the princess would know the protocol for such a situation.

The royal visit was also significant in that it planted the seed for what has become an enduring and respected institution associated with Høstfest: the Scandinavian-American Hall of Fame. A special banquet had been arranged to honor Princess Astrid during her 1983 visit—a banquet that proved to be so successful that organizers wanted to duplicate it the next year. The result: the inaugural Scandinavian-American Hall of Fame Banquet, held October 19, 1984, and highlighted by the inductions of Sondre Norheim, the father of modern skiing; Casper Oimoen, a champion skier who captained the U.S. Olympic Ski Team in 1932 and 1936; pilot/explorer Carl Ben Eielson, the first person to fly nonstop over the top of the world; North Dakotan Brynhild Haugland, who, at her retirement, was the longest-serving state legislator in the nation; and, of course, Myron Floren.

The early 1980s further marked the beginning of an important (and also enduring) trend for Høstfest—performances by entertainers direct from Norway, Sweden, and the other Nordic nations. In 1982, Høstfest discovered a Norwegian singer who would become an institution at the festival. Bjøro Håland, a smooth-voiced singer from Kristiansand, took the stage that year—and nearly every year since, he's been pleasing his loyal Høstfest fans with stylish treatments of old favorites and new works.

Carrol Juven, a Fargo travel agent and one of Høstfest's most loyal supporters, coordinates appearances by artists and groups from Scandinavia, and said that Håland (in 1982) and the Skien Accordion Orchestra (in 1983) were the first important Norwegian acts to appear at Høstfest, thrilling the crowd and creating an appetite for more "direct-from-Scandinavia" talent.

Above: A crafter shows off his work.

Facing page, top: Stabbur (storehouse for grain, clothing and food— uniquely Norwegian) in Shirley Bicentennial Park.

Facing page, bottom: Statue of Sondre Norheim, the father of modern skiing, located in Shirley Bicentennial Park.

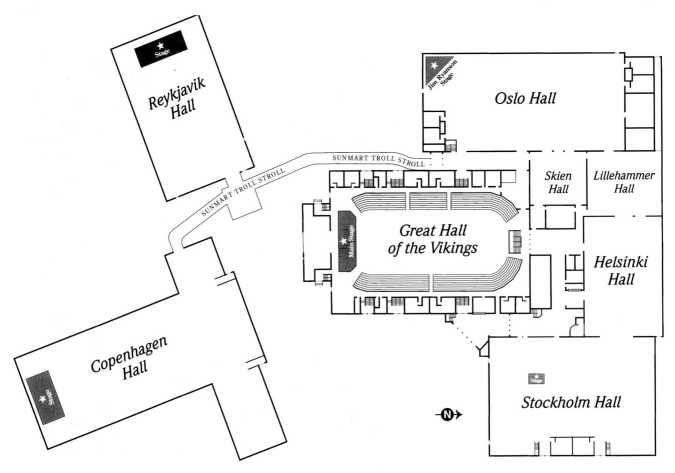

The involvement of Scandinavian acts continued to grow through the mid-1980s with repeat appearances by Håland, and the emergence of another fan favorite, family musical group The Liljedahls. Both acts helped to provide a true Scandinavian flavor to Høstfest entertainment—a flavor that festival patrons can't seem to get enough of.

While the quality and number of Scandinavian entertainers at Høstfest were increasing, so too were the attendance figures. And as attendance grew, the number of halls in which Høstfest was held grew as well: the Great Hall was joined by Skien Hall; then came Helsinki Hall, Stockholm Hall, Oslo Hall, Copenhagen and Reykjavik halls (honoring the capital cities of the five Nordic nations), and finally Lillehammer Hall, until the festival was covering more than 200,000 square feet by the early 1990s. With more space and more people (an average of more than 60,000 by 1991), the only thing missing was more time to enjoy it all. Høstfest expanded to three days in 1986, went to four days the next year, and hit its stride of five nights and four days in 1990. Bigger too were the *names* appearing on Høstfest's tickets. The Oak Ridge Boys, Red Skelton, Bob Hope, Barbara Mandrell, Victor Borge and others gave Høstfest the marquee value needed to attract people from a wider area than Minot, North Dakota.

People traveled hundreds of miles to cheer their favorite entertainers, but once inside Høstfest's Scandinavia, they marveled at the diverse atmosphere of a true festival. As Reiten puts it, "We knew we had to be more than another concert. There must be a deeper meaning." That deeper meaning is, in a word, heritage.

Left: Bob Gustafson stands ready to play a tune on his Swedish horn.

Below: Strolling musicians, members of the Harvest States Høstfest Accordion Club.

Above: The SAS (Scandinavian Airlines System) dancers.

Right: Olav Skoe from Skien, Norway, at the grave of Sondre Norheim.

Heritage
The Firm Foundation

Look up "heritage" in the dictionary and you'll find the phrase "shared meaning element." Perhaps Webster would have been wise to add, "perfectly preserved at Norsk Høstfest," because, more than anything else, heritage is what the festival is all about—and what sets it apart from other events. Heritage radiates from Høstfest's halls, originating in the cornerstones of the festival: food, clothing, music, friendship, and traditions of generations past. The aroma of authentic Scandinavian cuisine, the sight of traditional costumes, the sound of lively fiddles, the touch of a firm handshake—passing occurrences by themselves, but taken together, they are heritage coming alive.

At its core, Høstfest is a reflection of a tradition that festival president Chet Reiten remembers from his boyhood—a tradition brought from the small towns of Norway to new settlements in America that revolved around weekly social gatherings. Every Saturday night, people congregated in town, shopping, eating, seeing a show, and building friendships. That small-town Saturday night lives on again every year at Høstfest.

Reiten, a man who seldom contains his enthusiasm for anything, vigorously promotes Høstfest as a showcase for the values he and thousands of other Scandinavian-Americans hold so dear. He and many others who organized the first Høstfest are second-generation Norwegian-Americans. Their grandparents, pioneers of one hundred years ago, broke the virgin prairies, built sod houses, organized churches, started schools, founded small towns, and raised families. And while they were patriotic Americans, they were also very proud of their Norwegian heritage, which embraced faith in God, respect for others' rights, honesty, the work ethic, perseverance, and compassion. They instilled those values in their children and grandchildren, and the result is the strong ethnic pride so evident among today's Norwegian-Americans—the people most likely to show up at Høstfest!

What a difference a day makes

Høstfest's halls are filled with stories of people realizing the strength of their connection with Scandinavia. Consider Mark Hanson of Minot and his mother, Mabel Hanson of Larimore, North Dakota, both 100 percent Norwegian. For Mark, Høstfest was an awakening to his heritage. For Mabel, the festival was the catalyst that led to her discovering more about her ethnic background.

Mark, an editor for the *Minot Daily News*, knew little of his heritage until a trip to Høstfest sparked a chain of events that linked him solidly with his past. Accompanied by his mother, Mark learned part of his family's history that day (three of his grandparents were born in Norway) by simply observing her reactions to various aspects of the festival. It was Mabel's first visit to Høstfest—and seeing the foods, crafts, and clothing she hadn't experienced since childhood evoked emotional memories for her. Back at work the next week, Mark sat down at his computer terminal and wrote an article with newly-learned details about the Hanson lineage, which included these words: "Up to [our trip to Høstfest], I didn't care much about my heritage…as the day went on, the urge to learn about my ancestors grew."

Mabel's trip to Høstfest also heightened her interest in her genealogy. She sent a copy of her son's newspaper article to her cousin in Hamar, Norway, who responded with a long letter full of details about family history—names, dates, birthplaces, and anecdotes. Meanwhile, one of Mark's cousins in the U.S. who had seen the article wrote to thank Mark for prodding *her* interest in the heritage of the family. As a result, the Hansons hope to travel to Norway to walk the land that their parents and grandparents walked before coming to America. All

this—a man discovering a zest for his past, his mother filling in blanks of her family's history, and a possible family reunion linking relatives from two continents—from a one-day visit to Høstfest!

More Norwegian than Norway?

Ellen Lovdahl had moved to North Dakota from Norway only four years before the first Høstfest was held in 1978. Since then, she missed only one edition of the festival (she was in Norway) and said she will come back every year because of the special memories of life in Norway the festival brings. Lovdahl said the costumes, woodcarving, rosemaling, and crafts make Høstfest almost more Norwegian than Norway itself. She regrets that more Norwegians can't come to Høstfest, thinking that it might stir in them an interest in their past—an interest she believes is now often absent. But while Lovdahl wishes that others could experience Høstfest, *she* spends a few days roaming the halls each year because "my heart is set on Norway...Høstfest helps me grasp hold of my past."

Notice the phrase "more Norwegian than Norway." Lovdahl is not alone in that observation—Vibeke Mohr, who operated a booth set up by Skien, Minot's sister city in Norway, used the very same phrase in describing Høstfest. Mohr, whose 1993 visit to Minot was also her first trip to the U.S., believes the festival excels in preserving traditions and culture that people in Norway tend to take for granted and says Høstfest offers a great opportunity to Norwegians *them-*

Above: Lillian Espeseth of the Norway Lutheran Church receives an award from City Manager Rolf Haugen and Mayor Audun Kleppe, both of Skien, Norway.

Facing page: A participant in the daily Bunad *Show.*

Norwegian singing star Bjøro Håland and Høstfest royalty—Melissa Lane, of Minot.

selves to get into contact with their heritage. Amazing, isn't it, that a festival in the heart of North America should have such an effect on native Norwegians.

Whether they were born in one of the Nordic nations, have family trees reaching back to Scandinavia, or simply have an interest in the land of the Vikings, visitors to Høstfest can experience heritage in many ways. One of the longest running heritage-based events is the daily *Bunad* Show, spotlighting the traditional costumes of the five Nordic countries. A *bunad* is a festive, almost formal style of dress in Norway and, when Arlene Saugstad of Minot volunteered to get the show going in the first year of Høstfest, the show was aptly named since it featured costumes only from Norway. Her years of work helped the show become one of the biggest draws of the festival. During that time, although keeping the name *"Bunad* Show," the exhibition grew to include representative dress from the other Nordic nations: Iceland's *peysuföt* and *skaùtbùningur*, Finland's *puku*, Sweden's *folkdräkt*, and Denmark's *folke dragt*.

Janet Neuenschwander, who has headed the *bunad* style-show committee for more than a decade, said it showcases Nordic clothing exactly as it was more

Top: A big crowd gathers for a Høstfest show.

Above: Always ready for another delicious Høstfest meal.

Left: Bunad *Show.*

29

than 200 years ago. Owners of the clothing—in some cases families including husband, wife, and children—often serve as models showing the significance of various parts of the clothing and explaining how the costumes are made. A single costume may be worth three thousand dollars, making the owner especially proud to show it off. And judging by the packed house for each day's *Bunad* Show, many people are eager to affirm that pride.

Another daily tribute to heritage is the Parade of Flags, which for years was held in the Great Hall of the Vikings, and now is held in Copenhagen Hall. An invocation opens the ceremony, after which the flag of each Nordic nation—Norway, Sweden, Finland, Denmark, and Iceland—is paraded up the center aisle while the nation's anthem is sung. The Canadian and United States flags are also presented, accompanied by their respective national anthems until, at the climax of the ceremony, seven colorful flags adorn the stage in a patriotic precursor to the day's entertainment. Høstfest President Chet Reiten said he borrowed the idea for the flag ceremony from a festival in Decorah, Iowa, during which five young girls, each with a small flag, walked up onto a stage. Høstfest's version was added in the early years of the festival and has become a major draw for visitors each year.

Transamerica Expedition makes its arrival at Høstfest. Leading the way are (left to right) former Minot Mayor George Christensen, Oslo Mounted Policeman Tore Grindem, and Glen Hill.

Facing page: The Skein booth gives a tempting glimpse of Minot's beautiful sibling.

Heritage came alive at one Høstfest through an appearance by a group of Norwegians who had just finished a trip on horseback across America, retracing the route of Norwegian immigrants one hundred years earlier. The Transamerica Expedition began at what was, and still is, the gateway to the United States for many immigrants—New York City—on Norwegian Independence Day, May 17 *(Syttende Mai)*. The expedition followed a zigzag route westward through the Great Lakes region, the Midwest, and the northern Rocky Mountains, ending at the foot of a statue of Leif Eiriksson in Seattle on October 9, 1994 (Leif Eiriksson Day). Geir Petter Petterson of the Oslo Mounted Police rode most of the journey on a horse named in honor of Sondre Norheim.

The Transamerica group's cross-country journey didn't *really* end in Seattle. Only days after arriving at the Pacific Ocean, many members of the Expedition turned eastward (on wheels this time) and came to Høstfest, marking their arrival with a police-escorted horseback ride from a statue dedicated to Sondre Norheim at the center of Minot, to the Høstfest grounds a few miles away. The Transamerica Expedition included Høstfest in its itinerary because, said project leader Tore Henning Larsen, the festival is "the one American event which has really come across back in Norway. No single event in the U.S. has received as much media attention in Norway [as Høstfest]."

Høstfest began establishing personal ties with Scandinavia in the early 1980s when Carrol Juven, a Høstfest supporter from the start, convinced Reiten, then mayor of Minot, that establishing a sister city relationship with a Norwegian community would benefit the city and the festival. Juven set up Reiten's first trip to Skien in the county of Telemark in 1981.

Even though the visit was arranged in advance, Reiten remembers his feelings during the train ride from Oslo to Skien—how presumptuous that he, a total stranger, was about to try to persuade officials in a foreign country to establish ties with *Minot, North Dakota!* But he was received like royalty, gave an inspiring speech at a banquet commemorating his visit, and saw the start of a relationship that has, over the years, brought many people from Norway to Høstfest.

The sister-city relationship led to an exchange of statues between the cities in 1987 and '88, *and* helped Minot play a small part in the staging of the 1994 Winter Olympics. The common denominator: the man immortalized in the statues, Sondre Norheim. Norheim contributed much to the sport of snow skiing, most importantly the design of the modern ski binding. He was raised in Morgedal, about 60 miles from Skien, and is buried near Denbigh, about 45 miles from Minot. When Reiten discovered details of Norheim's life, including the fact that his burial location was virtually unknown in Norway, he became determined to set the record straight. He arranged for Princess Astrid, during her visit to Høstfest in 1983, to lay a wreath at Norheim's grave at the Norway Lutheran Church near Denbigh. Since then, a wreath-laying ceremony has been held annually at the grave site. Soon after the 1987 event, a life-size statue of Norheim was erected in Minot at the Shirley Bicentennial Park. Four months later in Morgedal in early 1988, an identical statue was unveiled at a ceremony attended by Norway's King Olav and an audience of thousands.

The Norheim statue in Minot now has a companion towering over it—a monument housing an eternal flame that was sparked by a piece of Olympic history. Weeks before the start of the 1994 Olympic Winter Games in Lillehammer, Norway, the Norwegian National Olympic Flame was lighted from the fireplace of a shanty situated on land where Norheim spent his boyhood days learning to ski. That flame was eventually merged with the official Olympic Flame—which, of course, had originated in Greece—but not before it had ignited a torch to be flown to Minot. North Dakota Governor Ed Schafer escorted the flame across the Atlantic to be used to ignite the Sondre Norheim Eternal Flame Monument, which shares center stage with the Norheim statue in Minot's Shirley Bicentennial Park.

Høstfest's connection to the Olympic Winter Games extended beyond the Sondre Norheim link thanks to Gerhard Heiberg, the Chief Executive Officer of the Lillehammer Olympic Organizing Committee (LOOC). Heiberg attended Høstfest in each of the two years prior to the Games. His reasons for coming were many, including promotion of the Olympics in a region brimming with Norwegian-Americans, and learning how the small town of Minot could so successfully stage such a huge event as Høstfest. If Heiberg could observe the volunteer spirit that helps Høstfest run smoothly, he could then put it to use in the tiny town of Lillehammer, which was about to stage a major worldwide event.

Høstfest played a small part in helping the LOOC raise funds when Eric Hilton (yes, of *those* Hiltons), a guest of Høstfest in 1993, paid an Olympian price for a unique Olympics T-shirt, one of 1,000 auctioned off in the days leading up to the Olympics. The $3,700 paid by the hotel corporation's vice president held up as the highest price paid for one of the shirts until the final one was auctioned on the streets of Lillehammer the day before the Games began.

Hilton was in Minot to participate in another aspect of the festival steeped in heritage: The Scandinavian-American Hall of Fame. The Hall of Fame, instituted in 1984, honors Scandinavian-Americans, such as Hilton, who have excelled in their chosen field. From WW II hero Knut Haukelid to football coach Bud Grant; from aviator Charles Lindbergh to business mogul Curtis Carlson; from golf club innovator Karsten Solheim to astronaut Buzz Aldrin; from former Vice President Walter Mondale to entertainer Victor Borge, the list of inductees represents a wide range of endeavor. In recent years, the Hall of Fame has broadened its scope to include the Humanitarian Award, which honors persons of any ethnic background who have contributed significantly to their culture (actor Earle Hyman and artist Fritz Scholder, for example), and the International Scandinavian Cultural Award, given to a Scandina-

Chester and the King

Høstfest President Chester Reiten remembers the late King Olav of Norway as a man who savored a good conversation and a good laugh. But Reiten had to break through the rather reserved demeanor of His Highness to discover those traits. His first royal encounter was during the King's early 1980s visit to Concordia College in Moorhead, Minnesota, when Reiten said King Olav did very little talking. But several years later, visiting Norway to participate in the 1988 unveiling of that country's Sondre Norheim statue, Reiten got to know the real man behind the "Kingly front." He did it by telling the King the old joke involving an argument over who discovered America—Leif Eiriksson or Christopher Columbus?

When Columbus stepped off the Santa Maria *after landing in the New World, the Indians greeted him by saying, "Er det du, Columbus?" (Norwegian for, "Is that you, Columbus?")*

Reiten said the King laughed heartily (even though he had surely heard the joke before) and the two went on to talk for more than an hour about many things, including the King's trip to Minot in 1939 when he was Crown Prince and, of course, Høstfest! Of King Olav, Reiten said, "He was a delightful person."

Don Karsky creates a Norwegian flag table runner.

vian citizen who has made important contributions to Scandinavian culture (Gerhard Heiberg received it in 1993).

While it's an ingredient that makes Høstfest more than just another concert, or a lutefisk dinner, or a craft show, the Scandinavian-American Hall of Fame Banquet has also grown into an institution that helps keep alive the heritage so important to millions of people. It's the epitome of heritage honored—and honoring heritage, after all, is the true purpose of Høstfest. Longtime exhibitor Frederick Gridley, who dresses in full Viking costume each year, summed it up well: "It's important to remember where you come from, for it is the beginning of all wisdom." Reiten would agree: "We want to make people aware of their roots, because when you are proud of where you come from, the nation will benefit."

Above: Oslo Hall, before the rush.

Facing page: Preparing the General Store.

Preparations

Long before the first visitor presents a ticket to be admitted to Høstfest, hundreds of people have invested thousands of hours of precious free time to prepare for the event. In fact, preparations for the next Høstfest begin as soon as the doors are closed on the current year's festival. The groundwork for each edition of the event is laid by a network of individuals and committees, all striving to make the next Høstfest the best Høstfest.

While Høstfest patrons are heading home from another memorable few days of rekindling their interest in heritage and enjoying the varied entertainment the festival has to offer, Høstfest President Chet Reiten is already on the phone, working to find out what talent is available for *next* October. The process of establishing an entertainment lineup actually begins during Høstfest, when patrons are surveyed as to which performers they'd like to see at future festivals. Several weeks and months are then dedicated to determining who has an open date, hammering out scheduling details, agreeing on compensation for the appearance, and finally signing the contract. This chain of events occurs for each of dozens of performers, from the headliners on the main stage to the Scandinavian groups that perform several shows on other stages over the course of four days.

While Reiten sweats over the details of setting an entertainment lineup, Pamela Alme Davy and Linda Bromley, the festival's only full-time, paid employees, are taking care of the myriad other tasks involved in preparing for the next Høstfest. But they are not alone—dozens of volunteers are also at work, providing the foundation for the building of another edition of "North America's Largest Scandinavian Festival."

The work of those volunteers, through committees, grows slowly but surely in intensity until summer rolls around and Høstfest is mere months away. Committees dealing with matters such as food, housing, and the media (fact: more credentials are issued to media representing Scandinavian publications and broadcast outlets than to their U.S. counterparts!) begin considering their tasks. It's also about summertime when the "supercommittee"—a group of key committee chairpersons—begins to hold regular meetings, geared to making sure all the necessary work is being done. Bob Horne, an executive with a local electric cooperative and longtime Høstfest volunteer, is a supercommittee member who says the group delves into every aspect of putting together the event except booking entertainment. Security, floor plan, coordination among the six stages, distribution of passes to the thousands of people volunteering during the festival

itself—all these details come under the direction of the supercommittee. By the time mid-October arrives, every individual committee will have its marching orders and be ready to turn those orders into an event worth attending.

But while the people who stage the festival may be ready for Høstfest, staff and volunteers must wait until the last possible moment to transform the All Seasons Arena complex itself into an oasis of Scandinavia. It's a last-minute job because of scheduling; the complex traditionally hosts, of all things, a *rodeo* only 72 hours before the doors open on the Høstfest's first night. That means some truly hectic work by hundreds of people beginning immediately after the last rodeo bull is herded out of the facility. In the Great Hall of the Vikings, tons of sand used as the footing for livestock are hauled away so the main stage can be constructed; in Stockholm Hall, the huge Swedish flags are hoisted into place in the rafters; workers assemble the General Store that will soon be vending cheese, meat, and other samplings from the Nordic nations; walkways (known collectively as the "Troll Stroll") that connect Reykjavik and Copenhagen halls to the remainder of the festival are being erected; and semi-trailer loads of miscellaneous equipment are being unloaded.

Throughout the complex, alterations large and small are made to ensure that the people who will soon come through the gates will imagine they've stepped into a colorful, far-off world where they can immerse themselves in the past. It's a huge undertaking, but one that is attacked with anticipation and exhilaration. Just as cooler temperatures and shorter days gradually cause leaves to turn brilliant hues each autumn, this mixture of planning and hard work turns a structure of steel and cement into a slice of Scandinavia every October—in the case of Høstfest, however, the transformation is measured in hours rather than weeks.

Above: The colors of Høstfest.

Top: Stockholm Hall takes shape.

Left: A Høstfest friendship in the making.

Facing page: Readying the Great Hall. Notice the two big screens on either side of the stage—they make every seat in the hall a front-row seat.

Above: Tony Bennett.

Facing page: The Nittedal Choir from Norway. They sang every day on the main stage.

In the Spotlight

Høstfest, with its huge crowds and reputation for top-notch stars, is a lot like a miniature Branson or Las Vegas or Nashville packed into a few days. Just as you'll find big names on the marquees in those popular entertainment destinations, you'll find Høstfest's lineup studded with several world-class entertainers each year. Tony Bennett, Lorrie Morgan, George Burns, Anne Murray and Chet Atkins are just a few of the names that have graced Høstfest ticket stubs. Høstfest President Chet Reiten said the festival's lineup must, in fact, be stronger than those of Branson, Vegas, or Nashville to attract people to the remote town of Minot.

Being stronger, to Reiten, means giving the people what they want—and to do that, he developed a system of surveying the Høstfest audience to *determine* what they want. While patrons are "oohing" and "ahhing" at the entertainment, Reiten is busy handing out questionnaires, asking everything from what entertainment is worthy of the main stage in the Great Hall of the Vikings, to which acts make Høstfest-goers want to spend time at the five other stages scattered around the complex. The information gathered from the surveys forms the basis for deciding which performers will be asked to return and which new entertainers will be sought out. Reiten says he doesn't let personal preference interfere with the process of setting the lineup. He relies on a handful of people for ideas on whom to go after, but in the end, "we rely on the polling of Høstfest patrons to decide who will appear."

Once Reiten has his sights set on a performer, the battles begin—the battle

The comedy team Tina & Lena perform in Stockholm Hall.

over fitting Høstfest into the desired act's schedule; the battle over convincing a major star to do two shows in one day (Høstfest offers an identical main-stage show twice each day with the exception of the first night); and the battle over how much money the festival can spend on one act. Perhaps the biggest challenge faced by Høstfest in recent years has been convincing the big-name acts to come at all. Reiten said it's tempting for entertainers to settle in a place like Branson—where their fans come to them—instead of hitting the road.

One major star who has been "hitting the road" for decades made a recent stop at Høstfest in the midst of a new round of world-wide publicity. Tony Bennett (who was just being "discovered" by the MTV crowd) came to Høstfest in 1994 and drew several standing ovations from a sellout crowd of fans—young and old. A few songs into his performance it was evident that Tony Bennett and Høstfest are a perfect match. His modesty ("I've had very good teachers along the way so I've been lucky"), gratitude ("Bob Hope found me in a Greenwich Village cafe and gave me my break—he's the greatest"), his sense of family ("My greatest pleasure is to have parents and children thank me and my music for getting them together") and, of course, his memorable music, endeared him to all.

An entertainer who has made a truly indelible mark on Høstfest is Danish co-

Above, left: Chet Atkins.

Above, right: Crystal Gayle.

Left: National Football League Hall of Famer Jan Stenerud. (He's also a member of the Scandinavian-American Hall of Fame.)

median Victor Borge. His repeat performances at the festival are no accident—the people love his humor and music and Høstfest's organizers love *him* and appreciate his attitude toward the event. Høstfest Executive Director Pamela Alme Davy said Borge has a friendliness and approachability that make him a delight to work

Myron Floren.

with. She also said Borge has a special feeling for Høstfest and has been willing to "go the extra mile" in many cases. For instance, just minutes after stepping off the main stage at his latest festival engagement, Borge obliged a Høstfest request for a cameo appearance at the Scandinavian-American Hall of Fame Banquet in progress across the street. Suffice it to say, "The Great Dane" had saved a few quips for that audience as well!

Along with the "red hot" stars of the day, Høstfest features such time-honored entertainers as Myron Floren, who himself has come to be as much a part of the festival as lutefisk and lefse. Floren's first trip to Høstfest was in the festival's second year and, except for one year when illness kept him away, he's been at every one since. Davy said Floren genuinely loves his fans, and related one incident that demonstrates this, beginning with her meeting his charter flight at 2:00 A.M. the day of his first performance. Knowing Floren's tight schedule, Davy had turned down a request from the family of a man hospitalized for cancer treatment. They had hoped Myron could personally visit their father, who was unable to make his usual trip to the festival. After precious few hours sleep, Floren caught wind of the request and insisted upon stopping at the hospital on his way to Høstfest. Davy said it was a touching scene as Myron Floren, complete with accordion, told the man, "I heard you couldn't come to Høstfest so I'm bringing Høstfest to you." The executive director said, "That's just the kind of guy Myron is."

Floren's philosophy regarding entertainment is simple—give the audience what it wants. It's a fundamental principle he learned from Lawrence Welk, on whose weekly television show Floren was launched to fame. Floren said he well remembers Welk's words of decades ago: "If we play things people know, we're on third base already. But if we play something unfamiliar, we're back at home plate." That's why the accordionist, who plays the main stage just prior to the day's headliner, can annually be heard squeezing out old favorites, including several patriotic pieces. Floren calls on a group of school-age singers to help him out on a few songs in each performance. Minot's Western Plains Children's Chorus enthusiastically lends its unified voice to pieces ranging from "Achy Breaky Heart" to "America the Beautiful." Backstage before the performance, Floren's love for children is obvious in his spontaneous chatter with the kids. "Sure beats workin'," he said. The students returned the affection with laughs and attention as Floren mused out loud, "I wonder what we're going to perform next year?" That too is "the kind of guy" Floren is—always looking to the future.

Norwegian entertainer Bjøro Håland's history at Høstfest has many parallels to Myron Floren's. Since his first appearance at Høstfest in 1982, Håland has been one of the festival's most popular singers. His velvety voice, warm smile, and audience rapport make it easy to understand why he's so popular. Davy believes that, like Myron Floren, Håland is emotionally attached to Høstfest. A few minutes with the singer confirm this. He said Høstfest gives him strength to keep going with his touring and recording the rest of the year. "I can get goose bumps on my arms or tears in my eyes just looking at the things here. It's fantastic." The warmth of the crowd is like none other, said Håland. And the warmth continues after he's left the stage; just watch the crowd gather as he stops at a Musikk Butikk to sign autographs, or witness a fan giving a life-size poster of Bjøro Håland a hug while a friend snaps a photo. Like Floren, Håland said he hopes to keep coming back to Høstfest year after year.

Above: The Chmielewski Funtime Orchestra provides high-energy music.

Top: Bjøro Håland.

The enthusiasm for talent "live and direct from Scandinavia" is not reserved only for Håland—fans line up daily to experience other Nordic acts as well. The Liljedahls are one of the most popular singing groups to come to Høstfest from across the Atlantic. They became the first Swedish entertainers to perform at Høstfest in 1984, and their frequent appearances traditionally attract a big crowd for two or three shows per day. Other Scandinavian performers have established themselves as favorites as well: Steinar Albrigtsen, one of Norway's top country singers; Lindesnes Trekkspillklubb, a 30-member accordion band from Norway; Tor Endresen, a vocalist who has appeared often on *DaCapo!*, Norwegians' favorite TV variety program; and *DaCapo!* itself have all captivated Høstfest crowds.

The hosts of *DaCapo!*, Gunvor Hals and Vidar Lønn-Arnesen, say that because sing-alongs are a big part of their shows, they love the happy and outgoing people they encounter at Høstfest. Hals and Lønn-Arnesen rave about Høstfest as a terrific place to videotape their television programs, which are later broadcast on NRK (Norway's noncommercial channel) during the Christmas season. As you might suspect, there is normally no evidence of the holidays in Minot in

October. But one local family rushed the calendar a bit, stringing Christmas lights and gathering neighbors to sing Christmas carols for the *DaCapo!* cameras to record. "That's the people of Minot," said Hals, "They decorate their home for Christmas in *October* just for us!"

As you can see, even the entertainers who appear on stage are aware that there's something special going on at Høstfest. The warmth of the audience, the wholesomeness of the festival, and the general atmosphere convince many entertainers that trekking to

Above: DaCapo! *tapes a program to be televised in Norway.*

Facing page, top: Dancing up a storm.

Facing page, bottom: The Bulla Family performs.

Minot is well worth the effort. Two-time Country Music Association Entertainer of the Year Barbara Mandrell knows the feeling. Appearing on Høstfest's stage one year, she called up from the audience a man from Coon Valley, Wisconsin, and, after singing him a love song (while sitting on his lap and draping her hot-pink boa across his shoulders), Mandrell told him that she has bragged to many people about Høstfest "because it's so wonderful." (His response: "You wouldn't *believe* what I'm going to tell people about this place!")

Superstar comedian Bill Cosby has *also* talked about Høstfest (where he has twice performed) in other settings. Appearing as a guest on CNN's *Larry King Live*, he took a call from a viewer in Lillehammer, Norway, but before the caller could ask his question, Cosby interrupted, "Are you coming to Minot, North Dakota? All the Norwegians come to Minot."

Whether Norwegian or of another background, Høstfest audiences seem to love family acts. Especially popular is a festival regular—the Chmielewski Funtime Orchestra, a Minnesota group that excites the crowd with a mix of listening and dancing music. It's easy to find a Chmielewski performance at Høstfest—just look for the people dancing in the aisles! Other family groups inspire dancing as well—one member of The Dutton Family, of Utah, has been known to search the crowd for a dance partner of his own. And Tennessee's The Bullas features musical prodigies of all ages, from Mom and Dad down to the youngest fiddler in the family who, by the way, is the *bunad*-clad sweetheart pictured on this book's cover.

While the music of The Bullas, The Chmielewskis, The Dutton Family, or other performers often moves Høstfest patrons to dance in front of the stages, there's also a more official way to kick up your heels—at the nightly Høstfest dance. After a day of walking, shopping, eating, and watching entertainers, hundreds of Høstfest-goers have energy left over (incredibly) for dancing to some down-home music. Even those who come unescorted are guaranteed a good time— each night, the nearby Minot Air Force Base sends in the troops (with rhythm, of course) to ensure dance partners for all.

Even as you walk from place to place within the festival, entertainment will find you, thanks to strolling musicians. In one walkway, an accordionist from the Harvest States Høstfest Accordion Band greets you with a smile and a spirited rendition of "Saturday Night Waltz," while in the middle of one of the festival's halls, a quartet including fiddlers and accordionists attracts a crowd with its impromptu concert.

If you're getting the impression that Høstfest is one big party, you're on the right track. The merriment can be found on stage, in front of the stage, and in every nook and cranny of the 200,000-square-foot festival grounds. Taken together, the entertainment at Høstfest is a grand show rivaling any to be found in Tennessee, Missouri, or Nevada. As one festival patron put it, "It's the best all-around entertainment you can find anywhere."

Above: Mmm! Good!

Top: Huge murals brighten Høstfest halls.

Right: Sev Brekke offers specialty cheese at the General Store.

Facing page: Terje Torgersen, chef from the Flamingo Hilton in Las Vegas, doing what he does best in the Norwegian Kitchen.

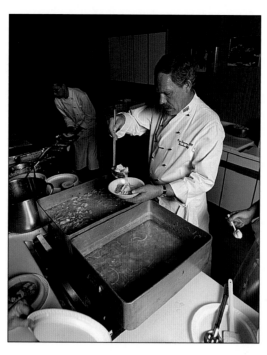

Food Glorious Food

It's April in Minot, North Dakota. Winter has lost its grip and spring flowers are beginning to blossom. People are resuming warm-weather activities—golf, tennis, jogging. Mike Nelson enjoys the spring as much as anyone, but his mind is also on autumn, specifically October. Nelson is in charge of food at Norsk Høstfest, and even though it is only April, the job of planning Høstfest's menu and securing every food vendor, chef, and food supplier begins now, six months before the aromas of Høstfest will waft through the All Seasons Arena complex. The huge volume of planning required with regard to food at the event was a surprise to Nelson when he took over the job in 1994. But, he said, he knows the work pays big dividends: "My goal is to have food be as important to the festival as is the entertainment."

Achieving that goal involves more than just stating a dream. It means phone calls, letters, faxes, meetings, and negotiations beginning months prior to the festival. Nelson must get commitments from people who want to provide food, negotiate acceptable terms for their involvement, decide which booths go where, and make sure the facilities will be ready come October.

Once the calendar reads "October," it's crunch time for Nelson and his committee. All Seasons Arena must be made ready for the more than 60 food operations that will soon arrive. While others are busy changing the look of the complex, the food committee is trying to change the taste and smell of the place (after all, a rodeo just ended!). That means getting food preparation areas cleaned and wired with the required power outlets, and bringing in ovens, cooktops, cabinets, and work areas so that every food vendor will be ready to cook when the doors open on Wednesday, the first full day of Høstfest. By the time Wednesday noon rolls around, the complex will have the aroma so familiar to Høstfest-goers—a mix of county fair and Christmas at grandma's—the aroma that takes them "home" again.

Let there be lutefisk...

In the beginning, there was lutefisk and lefse (and it was good!). Seriously now, from its very start, Høstfest cuisine has featured the most lasting culinary legacies of the Norwegian immigrants: lutefisk and lefse. The foods have be-

come a tradition today for Norwegian-Americans, partly because they are the foods that helped their ancestors survive the migration west after arriving in the new land 100 years ago. Lutefisk, which is dried codfish that is soaked in lye and boiled until flaky (sounds yummy, doesn't it?), was easily transported by the immigrants and provided many a nutritious meal. Lefse, which is potato dough rolled flat, baked, and served rolled up with butter (and sugar for those with a sweet tooth), was important for the same reason—it's compact, yet tasty and healthful. It was

Above: Lutefisk.

Right: Lefse.

only natural that two foods so important to the settlers would become the center of many of the family's special meals, such as holiday celebrations. It also follows that the foods would become the centerpiece for a festival dedicated to preservation of Scandinavian heritage. And even now, as the festival rounds out its second decade, those foods are the staples of what's offered to hungry patrons at Høstfest. Every year, more than 5,000 lutefisk meals and 50,000 slices of lefse are served during the four full days of the festival.

Lutefisk and lefse are to Høstfest what hot dogs and peanuts are to baseball games—the event just can't be fully enjoyed without them. But of course, the choices at the festival go far beyond those two favorites. Try the Finnish stew known as *mojakka; vinaterta,* a layered cake from Iceland; a steaming plate of mashed potatoes and Swedish meatballs; a piece of good old American fried chicken; or pies, pastries, and juices. And save some room for one of the delights offered today, as they were at the first Høstfest in 1978, by local churches: *røm-*

megrøt (cream and sugar topped with cinnamon) served by First Lutheran Church, rice pudding from Augustana Lutheran Church, *potet klubb* (dumplings) fresh from the Christ Lutheran Church stand, or *søt suppe* (sweet soup) sold by Bethany Lutheran Church.

Over the years, old favorites have been joined by new food choices. In 1991, a new tradition began with the opening of the Norwegian Kitchen, sponsored by the Norwegian Trade Council, Norwegian Seafood Export Council, and Hilton Hotels. In its first year, the Norwegian Kitchen served about 75 meals daily. That volume has ballooned to nearly 1,000 meals per day as patrons have discovered the delicious new foods being served. The Norwegian Trade Council and Norwegian Seafood Export Council provide food for the Kitchen, while Hilton Hotels sends some of its top chefs to staff it. Terje Torgersen, currently the head chef at the Flamingo Hilton in Las Vegas, arrives a few days prior to the festival to coordinate the setup of the kitchen and to train the workers who will help prepare the food.

Among those who work in the Norwegian Kitchen are young chefs and student chefs from around the world, seizing a chance to learn from a celebrated pro new ways to prepare and present gourmet foods. In one corner of the preparation area a chef fashions a thin salmon filet into the shape of a rose to put the finishing touch on a plate of seafood. Meanwhile, at the stove, overseeing the operation, Torgersen stirs the stock that will be used for a delectable fish soup. While he carefully skims the fat from the top of the vat, he talks about the festival that's won his heart. "This is the only working trip I take each year. I love coming here because all of the people are so nice." The native of Stavanger, Norway, who moved to the United States in 1975, stirs more fish and vegetables into the stock as he chats with a prospective diner. And the reviews from one of the first customers to dine on the seafood special? "Outstanding. I'll probably be back tomorrow for the soup."

That satisfied customer intends to return, but she could very easily become

How's that again?

Høstfest. It seems an easy enough word to say. But a walk around the festival will prove to you that there are nearly as many variations on the pronunciation as there are calories in that dish of rømmegrøt *you're eyeing. The problem, you see, lies in that small diagonal line passing through the letter 'o.' That changes it from the standard 'oh' sound to something closer to...well, it's nearly impossible to put on paper! Assuming you can say the word 'fest' with no problem, here are some examples of what 'Høst' should* not *sound like:*

Host (rhymes with most)

Hoost (rhymes with roost)

Hoost-ah (rhymes with rooster as spoken by someone from New Jersey [joy-zee] Note: this one also violates the two syllables only *rule!)*

Now, we offer our best attempt at explaining how it should sound:

Hust (rhymes with must, but with just a hint of the 'oo' as in cool)

or

Hust (as in the vowel sound from the word 'foot')

By the way, in writing Høstfest, always remember to put the slash through the 'o'. If you don't, a Norwegian may think you're referring not to a fall festival, but to a coughing festival!

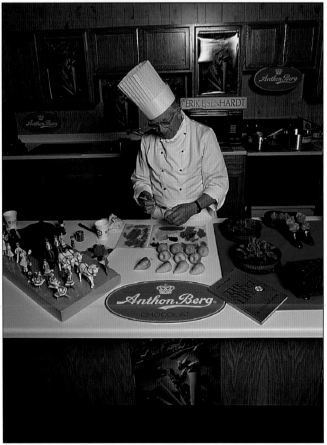

sidetracked in coming back "for the soup." After all, she's likely to walk past the *Danish* Kitchen with its gourmet chocolate delights. Mike Nelson said the Danish Kitchen was a big hit in its first year in 1994, and it's growing. Its chef, the top confectioner in Europe, Erik Ejsenhardt, wowed crowds with his chocolate sculptures. Working on a table brimming with examples of his work (the royal coach complete with horses was incredible—and edible!), he kneads a piece of marzipan, a moldable almond candy, into a ball and then flattens it out before gently curling it into a tube. As people begin gathering, Ejsenhardt takes a second piece and a third, fanning them out until it's suddenly obvious what he's crafting—a completely edible rose. Several petals later, the rose is ready to sit atop his latest piece of work, a candy box that not only *holds* chocolate, but *is* chocolate. The artist/chef says he had no formal training—only a job with SAS Airlines and a directive to make special gifts for VIPs flying with the airline. The result was a career that has spanned decades, and a long line of satisfied and amazed customers (apparently, necessity *is* the mother of invention!). The Danish Kitchen is sponsored by Anthon Berg Finest Chocolates of Denmark, and Nelson said its products (sold at the kitchen) were so popular that first year, the entire stock was sold out the first day of Høstfest.

Ejsenhardt and Torgersen are not the only chefs demonstrating their craft at Høstfest—Ingrid Espelid Hovig, "Norway's Julia Child," attended a recent festival. She's a regular on Norwegian television, offering recipes and cooking tips. At Høstfest, Hovig was cooking up some of her favorite foods, including brown bread. "It's wonderful because it has fiber, iron, vitamins," she said as she prepared a loaf to bake, "and it's so good—very tasty."

Scattered among the specialty kitchens and church food booths are dozens more taste sensations from the Nordic nations and just about everywhere else. Want the best coffee in the state? Check out the Hills Bros. booth or mobile coffee carts. Like to try some sardines? Sample the King Oscar Sardines available at the General Store. Hungry for some chili? Try the Chugwater Chili offered by folks from Chugwater, Wyoming. (You *may* decide the name refers to what you have to do after each bite of the spicy concoction.) Feel like beef? Test the barbecued beef sandwich at the Ultimate Rib booth (your authors did—delicious!). How about some of those famous Swedish meatballs? Or, experiment with a gyro (pronounced "hero" with a roll of the 'r'), a delicacy that the booth's proprietor said comes from *southern* Norway (he claims the Vikings would come to Greece just to enjoy it). There are dozens more choices—so many, in fact, that it could become a question of how many meals one can fit into a single day.

Above: Some of Ejsenhardt's chocolate creations.

Facing page, top: "Let me at that lutefisk!"

Facing page, bottom: Erik Ejsenhardt creates another edible masterpiece.

Of course, you won't have to eat standing up at Høstfest. Tables are placed all around the major dining areas, and they're arranged based on one assumption—when you're among friends, you like to *talk* while you eat. That's why the tables are situated cafeteria-style—you can comfortably chat with an old friend, or make a new friend while enjoying your food. And with so many exciting and interesting foods to try, you'll find yourself seated at one of the dining tables several times each day, befriending new foods and nourishing new friendships.

The explosion in the numbers of food choices at Høstfest has been by design. Nelson said his committee is always working to improve the variety and presentation of foods, whether they're prepackaged (such as the specialty cheeses at the General Store), or prepared on site. He believes that although entertainment often brings people to the festival the first time, the pleasure of getting together and celebrating heritage keeps them coming back, and food is a key ingredient in that celebration.

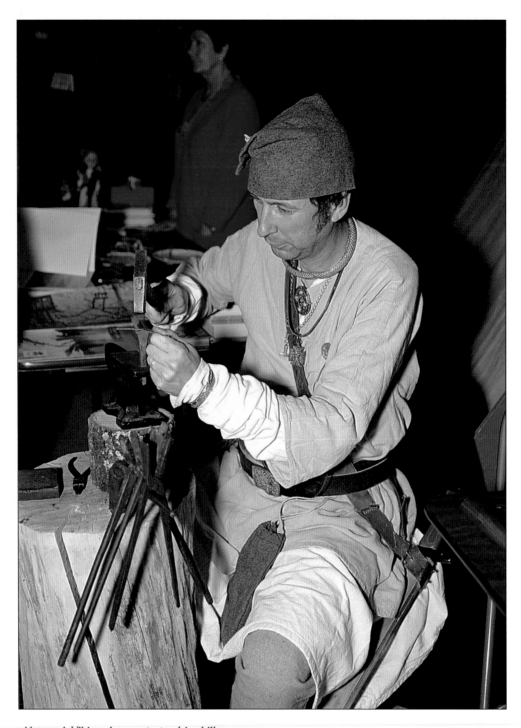

Above: A Viking demonstrates his skills.

Facing page: In keeping with the style of the day.

Treasures of Tradition

Remember that "small-town Saturday night" tradition—where friends would gather each week to mingle, eat, and see a show? Another part of the get-together was shopping—and Høstfest carries forward that tradition on a grand scale. In fact, many patrons would admit that it's the chance to "power shop" that brings them through the door in the first place! Hundreds of merchants come from near and far to participate in what Høstfest labels the Viking Market—the largest collection of specialty goods found under one roof for hundreds of miles. The shopping selection includes everything from finished items brought to the festival, to crafts and gifts created on site. For several years, Sharon Klusmann has coordinated the approximately 120 exhibits, and said she has tried to offer a blend of the familiar (rosemaling, woodcarving) along with the new (how about computer-assisted quilt making?).

While Klusmann said she strives to offer Høstfest patrons a diverse collection of merchandise, she follows one hard and fast rule. "We want to be faithful to Høstfest's 'heritage' theme, so everything must have a Nordic flavor—this is not an arts and crafts show." While that may sound like a limitation on what you'll see during a stroll through the Viking Market, rest assured that the selection is so diverse, the only "limit" you'll be concerned about is the one your credit card company imposes!

Who needs a mall?

Allow your authors now to take you on a Høstfest shopping tour, beginning with a look at a perennial favorite of the festival: sweaters. But these are no ordinary sweaters—they are nothing short of works of art. Most sweaters found in Høstfest's Viking Market are made of pure Scandinavian wool and come in virtually all colors and styles. Jim Johnson of Minneapolis, who operates Scandia Imports, boasts about his selection of Norwegian sweaters: "100% hand-knit in Norway with wool that will last a lifetime." Johnson says Høstfest is a great market for his sweaters. One look around and you can see why—it seems *everyone* is either wearing one or is purchasing one. You can expect to pay $150 to $300 for a quality Scandinavian sweater at the Viking Market. By the way, Høstfest is soon hoping to capitalize on this "sweater fever" in a unique way—with a likely attempt at becoming listed in the Guiness Book of World Records. The category? "Most People Wearing Norwegian Sweaters Under One Roof."

Oh! Those Norwegian sweaters!

While we're looking at clothing, how about trying on a pair of Swedish clogs? Båstad Clogs are made in southern Sweden and, we're told, are selling like Swedish hotcakes. The clogs may look clunky, but once your feet have experienced their world-renowned comfort, you'll be hooked.

Not far away, a man from Minnetonka, Minnesota, is selling Christmas ornaments (with a Scandinavian theme, of course) designed and created by his wife. In the same hall, Jean Odden of Barronett, Wisconsin (blink and you'll miss it, she said) offers everything from trolls to *bunads* imported from Oslo. Next stop, an award-winning booth called Mumbling Stumps. Sue Vogen from Two Harbors, Minnesota, offers six styles of wooden boxes she made herself (bruises on her hands prove it). Why the name "Mumbling Stumps?" "Because they're not whispering pines," deadpans Vogen.

For a change of pace, let's stop at the Høstfest Bookstore. It stocks a bit of everything, from novels to narratives, cookbooks to joke books, and even greeting cards. One recent year, many Høstfest patrons did a double-take, seeing two former governors side by side promoting their works. Former North Dakota Governor Bill Guy's book, *Where Seldom is Heard a Discouraging Word,* is a compilation of anecdotes and stories from his public life over several decades. Former South Dakota Governor Joe Foss is featured in a book entitled *A Proud*

American, written by his wife, Didi. Foss is a highly-decorated WW II flying ace who went on to become one of his state's most popular chief executives.

One shopping experience not to be missed is the Import Shop, a huge market operated by Høstfest itself, and offering a wide range of items: Nordic sweaters, authentic Norwegian-style felt hats, Porsgrund china from Norway, to name a few. The organizers of the Import Shop are constantly combing the international market to offer Høstfest shoppers new choices each year.

Next on our shopping list is jewelry. Dozens of merchants offer everything from pins

made especially for Høstfest featuring a Norwegian flag and a Viking, to the traditional fine jewelry of Norway known as *sølje* (one rarely sees a *bunad* without an accompanying piece of *sølje*). In one popular *sølje* booth, Kristin Mikkelborg of Norway displays the artist's touch needed to create a piece of the shimmering jewelry. While a crowd gathers, she carefully bends the silver, forms the silver jewels into their proper shapes, and cools the finished product for shoppers to admire.

Above: The Høstfest bookstore offers great variety.

Top left: "Wooden" you like a Høstfest memento?

Top right: Perusing the Nordic Newsstand.

Works in progress

In nearly every one of the festival's halls, you can observe artists in action as they create their crafts. Beautiful jewelry, woven tablecloths, carved chairs, intricate needlework—see them all "made from scratch" at Høstfest. In many cases, the demonstration includes wood—wood worked into everything from toys to storage boxes. Phillip Odden is a Wisconsin woodcarver who, on this day, is fashioning a basswood log into what he calls a Norwegian log chair. As he delicately carves out the circular pattern on the chair, Odden talks about the festival

Phillip Odden crafting a log chair.

that he's attended nearly every year, noting that over the years the crowd has become more informed about traditional Scandinavian crafts. Odden raises his voice to be heard over the singing of Norwegian superstar Steinar Albrigtsen from a nearby stage, and tells onlookers that he puts in an average of 80 to 100 hours making one of these chairs. A few feet away, a massive but intricately-carved door leans against the wall. Odden worked for two years putting what appears to be a thousand feet of carved pattern onto the 15-foot-high door, which will one day become one of two portals for a replica of a *stave* (traditional Norwegian church) planned for Minot's Shirley Bicentennial Park.

Not far away, schoolchildren hover around a loom operated by Don Karsky of St. Croix Falls, Wisconsin. Karsky, who gave up a career as a drummer to devote all his time to weaving, compares operating his loom at Høstfest to being on stage in a band. "My showmanship often got me hired as a drummer, so weaving for a crowd wasn't a big leap." Showman, indeed: as his loom comes to a stop, Karsky quips, "I've come to the end of my rope—there's not much weft." The students laugh as he reloads his loom to create more table runners bedecked with colors of flags of Nordic countries. Incidentally, Karsky bought his four-harness loom at an auction for $2.50 (!) back when weaving was still just a hobby for him.

Perhaps the most popular craft you can observe in the making at Høstfest is rosemaling, the painted circular floral pattern that is so...well...*Scandinavian*. While rosemaling is now considered a craft, it was, in a sense, a necessity to people of Nordic nations hundreds of years ago. Having few material resources at hand but still wanting to decorate their homes, they painted flowing, circular designs on wood pieces to be hung on a wall. The painted design became known as rosemaling or rose painting. Then, as now, certain designs were identified with particular geographic areas where popular. At one booth, Ann Schultz of Rochet, Minnesota, uses a steady hand to paint brightly colored designs on a wooden plate—the Rogaland style of rosemaling, she explains, named for the

Norwegian area where it originated. Rosemaling at Høstfest also can be found in some unusual places: Minot car dealer Jim Ryan (a good Irish-Norwegian) has given away vehicles with a one-of-a-kind, rosemaled paint job (cars seldom lost in the mall parking lot); and entire walls at Høstfest have become rosemaled murals. One visitor from Norway, after observing the variety and prevalence of rosemaling at the festival, predicted that any revival of rose painting in Norway is going to come from the American Midwest rather than from within Norway itself.

Tatting is also demonstrated at Høstfest. Like rosemaling, the roots of this craft go back to early Scandinavia, when it was developed for decorative purposes. Tatting is done using thread and a shuttle to produce delicate, airy, lace-like cloth. Judith Lind, a Høstfest award winner for best demonstration craft, says people are quite interested in watching her tat. That's confirmed by the large number of spectators often gathered 'round. She says it's "a little tricky but I know how to do it!" Oh—did we mention?—Lind is 90 years old!

Above: Julie Karsky displays the fruit of Don Karsky's loom.

Top: The Import Shop has a bit of everything.

Evidence that Høstfest is always looking to the future is found at our next stop—a booth featuring what could best be described as "high-tech quilting." The woman busy cutting out pieces for her next quilt explains that the templates she's using as a guide were computer-drafted and laser-cut. She simply puts the templates onto the cloth, slices the material with a rotary cutter, and sews the pieces together. Time required to produce one beautiful, full-sized quilt? As little as one hour!

Our shopping trip wouldn't be complete without checking out Høstfest's official art print, an annual tradition begun in 1994. Norway's Sigmund Årseth, a veteran Høstfest exhibitor, provided the painting used for the first year's poster—a richly-colored view of his front porch at sunrise. Årseth said the joy of his daughter's and grandsons' arrival the night before he painted "On the Doorstep" was his inspiration for the work. He explained that he thought, "I won't go any farther than my front doorstep" and he began capturing the view as the first beams of light illuminated the porch. He was finished with the work in a few hours—an average time for him. "I try to paint fast to catch the mood of the moment and the vividness of the colors." The 1995 Høstfest art poster is based on a

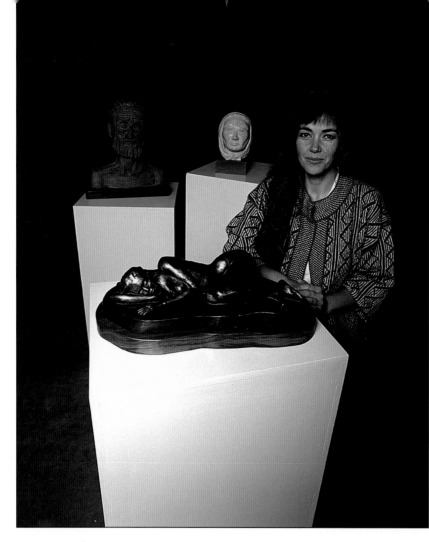

Left: Sculptor Tone Ørvik currently lives in Washington State but is originally from Norway.

Facing page, top: Nancy Jones Schafer, Sigmund Årseth, Chet Reiten, and Governor Ed Schafer with Årseth's "On the Doorstep."

Facing page, bottom: The phrase that says it all.

piece by Fritz Scholder, a North Dakota Native American whose work is loved and respected around the world.

If your taste in art leans more toward sculpture, take a look at the display presented by an artist who has an uncanny knack for capturing human emotions in clay. Oslo-born Tone Ørvik, who now lives in western Washington state, draws inspiration for much of her work from today's headlines of starving and mistreated people in Third World nations. For her display at Høstfest, however, Ørvik brought a cross-section of her work, including a bust of a woman she feels portrays the "determination and goodness" of the typical Norwegian woman. The sculptor says the festival has given her an opportunity to show her work to a new group of people.

As we've been shopping, you may have noticed all of the Vikings roaming around Høstfest. To many people, the craggy-looking characters symbolize the Nordic nations. In fact, a statue dedicated to Viking explorer Leif Eiriksson was unveiled in Minot's Shirley Bicentennial Park as part of Høstfest in 1994. Back in Stockholm Hall, Frederick Gridley, looking very much like a Viking explorer, operates a shop selling clothing, jewelry, and trinkets with a Viking theme. Ask Gridley why he comes to Høstfest each year and he breaks into his best Viking voice to joke, "To provision my ship, of course! Just look at all these people—heavy purses, much loot!"

The Viking Age Club of Minneapolis annually sets up a Viking encampment with reproductions of 10th-century tents, beds, and arts and crafts items. At one end of the display you can watch a Viking making chain mail, while at the other, you can hear how Vikings created colorful yarns using natural dyes such as onion skins and chrome. Of course, many of the items you see are for sale.

How about some more educational shopping? This time, we'll return to life as it has been for centuries for people native to northern areas of Scandinavia, the Sami. Høstfest has included crafts and displays depicting the life of the people you may also know by the name Lapps. Sami people have their own colorful flag (which was included in the daily flag ceremony), and are allowed to travel freely across the borders of Finland, Norway, Sweden, and northwest Russia. Susan Meyers, a descendant of Sami from Norway, says that while reindeer herding dominates the folklore of the Sami, only about 10 percent of the Sami people actually follow reindeer cross-country.

The Sami display includes live reindeer brought in by a man from Finland, Minnesota. Nearby is a *kota*, a tent used by Sami during the reindeer migration (although they now use snowmobiles and airplanes as well). Anja Kitti, whose family is from Kittiland, Norway, explains that the *kota* can be quite homelike, complete with a wood-fueled fire that is extinguished only at night. Kitti was born to Sami parents, but moved to Toronto when her mother sold off the family's reindeer after her father's death. She demonstrates for the crowd how Sami people prepare for a day in the land above the Arctic Circle. The most important detail is wrapping one's feet for warmth, using reindeer-skin boots stuffed with hay. Each boot is carefully secured to keep snow and cold out and body heat in—the same procedure that's been followed for centuries among Sami people. Visitors are not only able to watch such demonstrations, they may also purchase Sami crafts, foods (reindeer meat!), and publications.

Sculptures, paintings, rosemaling, jewelry, sweaters, books—as you can see, the shopping is splendid at Høstfest. Just watch that credit limit!

It's a small world after all

Høstfest was nearing, and my friend Jane Clark called, wondering if I would host an international guest whose visit she was coordinating. It happened that his visit fell during the festival, so I said, "yes," planning to have him tag along as I worked on the Høstfest grounds one afternoon. When I met Nils Ole Hilmer Torvalds at the ticket window and found out he was an official with the Finnish Broadcasting Company, I assumed he had timed his visit to coincide with the festival. I was wrong. Torvalds had simply come at this random time as part of a cultural exchange program. One of my duties that day was to do a television story on the Sami Village set up in Copenhagen Hall. As I was interviewing Anja Kitti, a woman born to Sami parents, Torvalds took notice of her distinctive style of clothing and her name. After chatting a bit, he realized he had, only weeks earlier, met and talked to a member of Kitti's family while hiking in Sami territory in northern Finland.

—Jim Olson

Above, left: Artist and sculptor Peter Esdaile, from Oslo, received an award for best demonstration in a booth.

Above, right: Rosemaling display.

Left: Stabbur in Oslo Hall, displayed by Bruce Meland of Bend, Oregon.

Above: Smiling is a usual Høstfest reaction.

Right: Smiling while dancing is a usual Høstfest action.

Facing page: A participant in the daily Bunad Show in Oslo Hall.

People
The Heart of Høstfest

Norsk Høstfest is a gathering of friends you just haven't met yet; that's how one volunteer sums it up. You'll hear many variations on that theme, all with one message in common: people make Høstfest happen.

"People I meet are 90 percent of why I keep volunteering each year."

"Høstfest is a way to reconnect with your heritage and enjoy people."

"Happy people enjoying themselves—that's Høstfest."

"It's my first time at Høstfest. I was amazed at the hospitality of the people."

"Every year, I make several new friends—people here are great!"

"People are so friendly and open here" (from a Norwegian visitor).

Høstfest President Chet Reiten sums it up: "Friendships developed at Høstfest are a key to getting people to come back. If they feel comfortable, they'll return."

The job of giving Høstfest that "comfortable" feel falls to the festival's most important people—its volunteers. Reiten is Høstfest's most visible volunteer—but he's only one of thousands who donate time. Most give a few hours during the festival itself, working at food booths, craft shops, ticket booths, RV parking lots, etc. But a special few actually volunteer on a full-time basis, spending many hours per week year-round working out details of the festival. In short, nearly everything that happens during Høstfest happens because of volunteers. As one helper said, "There's a real excitement in putting Høstfest together."

Right: Stepping out at Høstfest.

Facing page, top: Høstfest Executive Director Pamela Alme Davy (middle) and (left to right) Lt. Gov. Rosemarie Myrdal, Norwegian Ambassador Kjeld Vibe, Chet Atkins, and Minnesota Congressman Martin Sabo.

Facing page, bottom: A member of "Proffene," a group of Norwegian performers with developmental disabilities.

Making it happen

Exactly *who* volunteers to help at Høstfest? (With 8,000 volunteer passes printed each year, perhaps a better question would be...who *doesn't* volunteer?) They are people just like you, your friends, and your neighbors. People like Faye Arlt of Minot. Every year, just before the festival begins, she can be found painstakingly numbering a good portion of the more than 2,800 chairs set up on the floor of the Great Hall of the Vikings before the festival's opening night entertainment. Arlt's sister from Hamilton, Illinois, drives the 900 miles to Minot to donate her time to helping at Høstfest, also in the Great Hall. And yet another sister travels to Minot from Detroit Lakes, Minnesota, taking vacation time from her job to volunteer. Arlt's husband and three of her daughters also get involved in Great Hall work. They're all there—ushering, setting up, helping out—because, "it's so much fun. I get goose bumps before Høstfest even begins," Arlt says.

Volunteerism crests when Høstfest is actually staged, but even when the festival is several months away there's work to be done, and volunteers are ready and willing to do it. Indeed, almost the day after one festival ends and the next is nearly a year away, people such as Gladys Holter, Morris Lawrence, Helen Haaland, Ruby Crites, and Evelyn Anderson are back at work at Høstfest's year-round headquarters in downtown Minot's Norwest Bank building, donating many hours each week to keep the organization running smoothly.

With volunteers willing to work five or six days per week year-round, Høstfest, a multimillion-dollar operation, is able to thrive with only two full time, paid staff members. Executive Director Pamela Alme Davy may hesitate to do so, but must take credit for being the primary force in putting Høstfest into motion, planning nearly everything that happens. She seeks out and courts the corporate sponsors so crucial to the festival, develops new aspects to the event (the ethnic kitchens are a good example), lays the foundation for each year's Scandinavian-American Hall of Fame Banquet, and gen-

erally serves as an ambassador for the festival in her travels near and far—making contacts across the U.S. and in Scandinavia to keep Høstfest fresh and growing.

Right: Linda Bromley (standing) and volunteers at work during Høstfest.

Below: A display of finery.

Administrative Assistant Linda Bromley gets more into the nuts and bolts of what must be done to stage the event. She tracks income and expenses, works out details of sponsor contracts, and deals, either in person or on paper, with virtually every entertainer, crafter, or vendor who is planning to be at the festival.

Davy, Bromley, and a half-dozen-or-so volunteers keep things humming along at the Høstfest office all year. Then, on May 17 (*Syttende Mai*—Norwegian Independence Day), the date tickets for the festival go on sale, the hum becomes more of a buzz. Suddenly, it seems everyone who lives within 500 miles of Minot is either in the office or on the phone, wanting to reserve seats for his or her favorite shows. A second crescendo of activity begins when September rolls around—more volunteers, more phone calls, more ticket sales, more questions to be answered—until, in early October, the activity is at a fever pitch, and every inch of space in an office that once seemed roomy is, shall we say, in *lively* use. But not to worry—out of this controlled chaos will soon come, once again, another memorable event: the Norsk Høstfest!

The melting pot

Sixty thousand people attend Høstfest in a typical year. Sixty thousand friends you haven't met yet. But who are they, these visitors who come from as near as down the street and as far as Finland and Sweden and Denmark and Norway and Iceland? Let's meet a few.

Everything and everyone is cheerfully decorated.

• Bill from Spokane was here with his wife and about a dozen other people from Washington state. The couple have celebrated their anniversary (October 15) every year for most of the past decade with a vacation in their RV that includes four days at Høstfest. "You can't beat it," he said.

• Gordon from Alberta, Canada, was making his first visit to Høstfest. He said it's amazing, with something for everyone, young and old alike, and that he would "highly recommend it to anybody."

• Marla, from Minot, had been to many Høstfests. On this occasion, she was appearing in the *Bunad* Show and said, "Høstfest is a fun place to be."

• Two women, part of a group from Benson, Minnesota, stopped to say "hello" (you couldn't help but notice them—they were sporting hats with the color scheme of a Holstein cow). Their summation of Høstfest? "Awesome."

"Getting down" at Høstfest!

• A woman operating a craft booth said this was her second visit to the United States, but her first at Høstfest after hearing about the festival from friends in Norway. She noticed the atmosphere most, and, "All the people are so nice!"

Friends in waiting

With any luck, the message is now clear to you—people *make* Høstfest. But how do you meet one of these friends-in-waiting? Høstfest has made it easy with five simple words: Hi! Where are you from? A phrase you're likely to hear repeatedly as you roam Høstfest's halls, *Hi! Where are you from?* has become the traditional Høstfest greeting by design. It's a natural way to start a conversation with a total stranger, but it's also a way to win $100 cash!

It's like this. Every day of the festival, one or two people are secretly given a $100 bill to award to the first person who says to him or her, *Hi! Where are you from?* The friendly promotion is well publicized as, each day, Reiten announces from the stage of the Great Hall of the Vikings that by simply uttering the phrase to the person near you, you'll meet a wonderful person *and* could win $100. He said the buzz of five or six thousand people turning to greet each other is amazing.

But beyond the chance to win cash, Reiten said *Hi! Where are you from?* is successful because it starts a conversation often leading to an "I know someone who has relatives there" exchange—the seed of friendship that can easily grow. Friendships sprouting from *Hi! Where are you from?* commonly become long-lasting, branching out across states and countries and from one year to the next. "It's easy to see how lifelong friendships can be formed from those five words," said Reiten. By the way, even though you will often spot Reiten, in his *bunad*, roaming around greeting people at Høstfest, he does *not* have the $100!

Above, left: Høstfest is a "banner" time in Minot.

Above, right: Everyone is huggable at Høstfest.

Top: "And then Lena said…"

No room at the inn

People, people everywhere and not a room to spare. That might sum up the lodging crunch that hits Minot at Høstfest time. The city has about 1,700 hotel and motel rooms but, even combined with rooms at motels in nearby towns, that doesn't begin to accommodate the huge influx of visitors each October. Once again, though, *people* get the job done—in this case, the job of helping to provide every guest and Høstfest exhibitor and entertainer with a place to stay—through what is called the Høstfest Home Host program. For years, Home Host Coordinator Harriett Herigstad has acted as matchmaker, contacting hundreds of local residents who then open their homes to Høstfest visitors, sacrificing a piece of their privacy to accommodate "the homeless." Incidentally, guest and host often form a friendship—a bond that is, in many cases, strengthened in subsequent years through repeat visits.

RVers are right at Høst-fest's front door.

Another way around the hotel room squeeze is to bring your own lodging. Høstfest offers hundreds of hookups for recreational vehicles and caters to RV travelers by providing computerized reservations, friendly volunteers to help in navigation of the festival grounds, and a special hospitality area including displays of new RVs and the gadgets owners love. After all, if you're driving in from hundreds of miles away, you deserve some VIP treatment!

Random acts of kindness

The spirit of hospitality that marks Høstfest's Home Host program spills out into the streets each year during the festival—just ask Vidar Kvalshaug, a twenty-something journalist with the Norwegian entertainment magazine *Se og Hør* (See and Hear) making his first U.S. visit. Kvalshaug arrived a few days before the festival one year and decided to take time one day to walk from his hotel to Wal-Mart ("We have no such things as Wal-Mart in Norway"). Not understanding that he faced a trek of several miles, Kvalshaug set out, eager to see the truly American institution. About halfway to his destination and realizing the store was farther away than he expected, he stopped at a service station to ask directions. Service station owner Leo Jundt had earlier seen Kvalshaug walking along the street and from his appearance *knew* he was a visitor from Norway. So, when the Norwegian came into his service station, Jundt offered him a ride. Kvalshaug said that would be great, "if you're going that direction." Jundt fibbed and said he was and the two were off to Wal-Mart, leaving another worker to staff the service station. The act of kindness made a big impression on Kvalshaug (who thought Jundt had *closed down* his gas station to help). The journalist says he had been influenced by news reports in Norway of crime in the streets of America, "but coming to Minot is like being back in Norway—everyone is so friendly."

Jim Johnson of Minneapolis also discovered Høstfest hospitality in the streets of Minot. Johnson, a vendor who operates Scandi Imports at the festival, arrived with his wares at the All Seasons Arena only to realize he had lost a huge carton of woodcarvings. He retraced his route to the festival within the city, but could not find the box. Resigning himself to an expensive loss, Johnson began setting up his booth when a stranger approached carrying the carton. The good samaritan had seen the box fall from Johnson's truck and stopped to gather it and bring it to him at Høstfest. Johnson said the man refused a reward and he still marvels at his act of kindness, "I couldn't believe he went through all that effort to help someone he didn't even know."

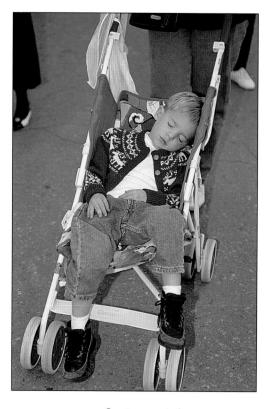

Getting ready for a second (third? fourth?) wind.

Brought to you by...

There's one group of people involved in Høstfest that, although small in number, plays a very large role in Høstfest: corporate sponsors. The list of sponsors of the festival is long and varied—from Super Valu to Trinity Medical Center, First American Bank to Northwest Airlines, Norwest Banks to Sunmart, Conoco to Scandinavian Airlines System. They, and many others, help "pay the freight," allowing Høstfest to gather such an impressive collection of entertainers, food, and crafts. In one case, a corporate sponsor helped place news of Høstfest into people's hands some 3 million times in the months leading up to the 1994 festival. Minot's Coca-Cola office arranged for the distribution throughout the Midwest of more than 3,000,000 cans of Coke emblazoned with the Høstfest logo and the dates of the festival. Manager Todd Wegenast of the local Coca-Cola office said being a corporate sponsor is good for everyone involved: the sponsor gets great publicity from the festival, and Høstfest gets promotion and money to help put on the show. Executive Director Pam Davy said Coca-Cola and indeed *all* of the corporate sponsors play a vital role in keeping Høstfest alive and well.

With all of the friendly people at Høstfest, you never know *who* you might encounter. In one hall, you could meet a woman who, you discover, knows family members of yours in another state; while doing some shopping in another hall, you might come across superstar Liza Minnelli perusing the merchandise (she picked up some jewelry at one Høstfest); sitting down to eat, you might find yourself across from Høstfest legend Myron Floren (who'd be happy to tell you about his experiences with Lawrence Welk); enjoying a show, you could hook up with an acquaintance you haven't seen since *last* Høstfest. In short, while you may come to Høstfest for the entertainment, the food, the shopping, or the chance to discover your heritage, it's the *people*—"the friends you just haven't met yet"—who are Høstfest.

Above: Wrapping up another Høstfest.

Right: Packing it away for next year.

Facing page: The job of disassembling begins.

Done Too Soon

    Standing in the middle of Stockholm Hall, one of Høstfest's busiest sites during the festival, it's hard to imagine the event ever ending. But, alas, all good things come to an end, and so it is with Høstfest. It's fitting that the climax of the festival is on a Saturday night, the night after which Høstfest is really designed. That final day always includes two shows by a top entertainer (Jay Leno in '95 for example), and, of course, Høstfest's one-of-a-kind blend of food, shopping, music, dancing, and socializing.

    As soon as the merriment has ended, the formidable job of dismantling this slice of Scandinavia begins. Once again, it's the volunteer spirit that sustains the effort, as displays are put away, stages are disassembled, decorations are stored, and semi-trailers of material are packed up for storage until next year. That such a large task is accomplished in a matter of hours is amazing; that the job is done with smiles and friendly words after days of too much fun and not enough sleep is, well, *Høstfest!*

    For Høstfest Executive Director Pam Davy, the end of the festival comes all too soon. After 51 weeks worth of work invested to stage the event, "it's done in a blink." Davy said the festival itself is a blur of activity and then, all of a sudden, it's over. "I hate it [when Høstfest ends]. I hate it when Myron [Floren] or Bjøro [Håland] gets on the plane Sunday morning to go home." Davy said if she could do anything drastic with regard to the festival, she would change Høstfest into a full one-week event. (Personally, we think it safe to assume that, no matter *how* long the festival, the executive director would hate seeing it end!)

Right: Farewell for another year.

Below: North America's Largest Scandinavian Festival regularly shows up on the American Bus Association's list of "Top 100 Events in North America," and apparently the list is widely read.

Facing page: Høstfest is a truly fun way to celebrate heritage.

The Høstfest Philosophy

Høstfest President Chet Reiten likes to say, "You have to create your own excitement, no matter where you are." Those words are perfect to describe Norsk Høstfest. It began as a small, friendly get-together, but grew (and grew), until today, this "get-together" can rightfully boast of being "North America's Largest Scandinavian Festival." It also regularly shows up on the American Bus Association's list of "Top 100 Events in North America." Reiten says that as the festival was slowly building a following of loyal patrons, it dawned on him, "This is a *big* thing!" But he shuns credit for making the event what it is today, claiming, "it was just an idea whose time had come."

Regardless of where credit is due, Reiten's statement is on target—Høstfest is a success because it serves a purpose, or many purposes, for people. It has entertainment, it has food, it has crafts, it has dancing, it has friends, and most of all, it preserves heritage. In a word Høstfest is synergistic—the whole is greater than the sum of its parts. Put another way, while each individual aspect of the festival would perhaps not flourish on its own, *together* they succeed, forming a true *festival*, offering something for everyone every day.

And what of the future? What will become of this prairie gathering of friends both known and unknown? Reiten said if the festival stays true to its real purpose—promoting heritage—Høstfest will continue long into the future. He

At home at Høstfest.

says people of all backgrounds are becoming more interested in their roots; older people pass on their interest in heritage to younger generations who, in turn, become wondrous about *their* heritage, thus providing a future audience for the festival. In fact, Høstfest's audience *has* been getting younger each year perhaps because of the festival itself—people who attend pass on their pride in heritage to their children—and the roots of Høstfest grow deeper.

When you ask Høstfest favorite Myron Floren what Høstfest is, his ever-present smile seems to broaden a bit: "It's my favorite place—I hope I can keep coming back here for another 25 years." Floren has participated in more than a dozen Høstfests, not only performing on the main stage, but also wandering the festival's halls alongside festival patrons and dancing a song or two with some. He said he's impressed at the gathering of people of many nationalities, particularly Scandinavian, to simply have a good time.

Floren's summation of the festival is perhaps the best we've found: "If the Høstfest philosophy could be spread around the world, we'd all have a lot fewer problems." Amen.

Above: Sweet dreams!

Top, left: Statue of Leif Eiriksson in Shirley Bicentennial Park.

Top, right: Any time is dance time at Høstfest.

Sondre Norheim Eternal Flame Monument.

Index

The authors are husband and wife of sixteen years, and the parents of two sons and a daughter ("works in progress"). Jim Olson, news director at KXMC-TV in Minot, has also produced two Norsk Høstfest Keepsake Videos. Lori Olson writes occasionally for Høstfest. The Olsons wish to thank Computerland of Minot for the use of a laptop computer in the writing of this book.

Clayton Wolt, a professional photographer based in Sterling, North Dakota, is a regular visitor at Høstfest.